A SYBIL SOCIETY

THE TEST SITE POETRY SERIES
Claudia Keelan, University of Nevada, Las Vegas, *Series Editor*

The Test Site Poetry Series is a collaboration between University of Nevada, Las Vegas's Black Mountain Institute, *Witness* and *The Believer,* and the University of Nevada Press. Each year, the series editor along with an advisory board, which includes Sherwin Bitsui, Donald Revell, Sasha Steensen, and Ronaldo Wilson, will select a winner and a runner-up. The selected winners will be published by the University of Nevada Press as part of this series.

Winning books engage the perilous conditions of life in the twenty-first century, as they pertain to issues of social justice and the earth. They demonstrate an ethos that considers the human condition in inclusive love and sympathy, while offering the same in consideration with the earth.

Refugia by Kyce Bello

Riddle Field by Derek Thomas Dew

Mouth of the Earth by Sarah P. Strong

A Sybil Society by Katherine Factor

Interior Femme by Stephanie Berger

A Sybil Society

POEMS

Katherine Factor

UNIVERSITY OF NEVADA PRESS | Reno & Las Vegas

University of Nevada Press | Reno, Nevada 89557 USA
www.unpress.nevada.edu
Cover photograph based on the *Priestess of Delphi* by John Collier

LIBRARY OF CONGRESS CATALOGING-IN-PUBLICATION DATA
Names: Factor, Katherine, author.
Title: A Sybil society : poems / Katherine Factor.
Other titles: Test site poetry series.
Description: Reno : University of Nevada Press, [2022]
Series: The test site poetry series
Summary: "In her debut collection, Katherine Factor excavates a post-patriarchal world with
  poems inspired by ancient oracles and goddess wisdom, mining time, ruins, and intelligence of
  past civilizations" —Provided by publisher.
Identifiers: LCCN 2021041598 | ISBN 9781647790400 (paperback) | ISBN 9781647790417
  (ebook)
Subjects: LCGFT: Poetry.
Classification: LCC PS3606.A263 S93 2022 | DDC 811/.6—dc23
LC record available at https://lccn.loc.gov/2021041598
The paper used in this book meets the requirements of American National Standard for
  Information Sciences—Permanence of Paper for Printed Library Materials, ANSI/NISO
  Z39.48-1992 (R2002).

FIRST PRINTING

Manufactured in the United States of America

For the ancestral dissidents

...we know not nor are known; the Pythian pronounces...

—H. D.

Apollo took it [the omphalos] from Ge, took the ancient
symbol of Mother Earth and made it his oracular throne.

—Jane Ellen Harrison

...the way to Hades is easy; night and day lie open the
gates of death's dark kingdom; but to retrace your steps,
to find the way back to daylight, that is the task.

—The Sybil to Aeneas, Virgil, *Aeneid* 6.125

Contents

A SYBIL SOCIETY

Aurora

Saved for when the lights went out.
The black they desired—the kind
Of blank that bellowed
Just before the new took place. Naked
As they were in the face. Aching for the show
For stellar, or better, any teeny bit of glow.
Look low on the horizon, dazzle-eye.
No ledge no ledge no ledge
Let's not grow but hurt instead?
The moment about to blow.

@the Last Venue

Having viewed & viewed   the fleet set out   tapping frets

Air slinking over   strings   so slippery   sound gated
   the promenade

Those prescient   entered the theater on an ember   eyes amber
   coupling a gel-lit sky

Chandeliers shined & chimed   in the backdraft   of the hush
   Come out of hiding

shower   the self w/brightness   Shouldering beams   spheres
   give off elegance

Crowds of ears slowed   rearing half-steps   roared perfection
   pulse as

in transmit   The keeping at heart   instructions from the anchor
   turned up

Attuning   we are   chromosomes   extracted from what's   dormant

When Medicine Comes for Us

We have waited in
the chamber
wailing for
hundreds of nights.
Resonating in
the resin
of hearing the piper play.

The vaccinated
left mirrors in their path—
a tubular past.
The spiral is
the migration story.

If we listen, we can hear
whispers of the worms
in the floor, wriggling just
to warn us, jotting through
the muddy funk.

Hurling discs waving flags,
letters are small bodies,
flagrant fingerprints
shooting up
from the amputations
unsure of what
is delivered next.

Best to let the alphabet
sail in. The sound
a pleasure dome.
The sound
a welcome storm.

White Goddess House

Boobs ignite   underworldly bulbs

then wake the rubble   & collate violet fertilizer

from our psychic eye   brigade

*   *   *

To keep from collapse   prepare the soil nominees

primp carrion wings   that feather a city

now decapitating the king   no prob

*   *   *

I get lit   when the bride   swaggers in

handsome seeds in the pendant

she's very expectant   a warmed-up
loam-mom

*   *   *

I knife you good I do   yet other harrowing seasons

contract me   once my night   is on track—

*   *   *

I unearth the calendar   &   hijack a palace

tonguing *we do magic*   while an archon

is sucked down   into this poem

A Sybil Society

So over these curious pilgrims—
untied to particular locations

                    we are onerous

yet we travail the countryside
offering psychic services for a small fee.

So that yr frat imagines—
a variety of methods at our disposal:

direct *enthousiasmos* aka trance obsession
dream interpretation   the casting of crap
dice or knuckleheads   to predict this

hella gratuitous reading

mimic the flight of birds
or the movement of sacred animals.

            My sisters   *sorry*
            we're all scrying

interpreting the emails
of sacrificial victims
then consulting certain message texts.

An Ariadne

Come to create
here   hear
a sound economy

where we wear
an axe   as access

whorl a red fleece
to seek & see

this place
all about being lost

but darn
a precocious thread in
a bull cabinet

& if he comes from
a long time ago
write a re-lease of me

ocean-floored crown
thrown up to vision board

in create
I am known in honey
I snake   the dead

on the ship
the youth repeat
throes of labor

the twine has an eye
yet nary a
needle meddles

I *ahhhh* maze
you   but if
left pregnant

I create
as all get out

as lady honey
of this palace

if we seed the speakers
I will comment again

cement the labrys
honor me

further   father
is a lightning guide

are you awake sire

I said to the dead bee
invited to the viewing

oh master octave
mind the freeway

to awake
one's ride

so what
if that sound
is all around

pearl purity
tread the treat

as trending codex
brackets a home

several pods
need my body

that denotes
a giving economy

also a number
of activities

at all times
in all entrances

an innocuous
meantime

so let's trample
maze lines

& just trust
if I am

seen writhing
it is official

Delphi Selfie

Ramrod   set up that tripod   while they quarry rubble

& develop strange rules   to create great   scholar wonder

at the vein gas earth talk   it tickles   until nonsense mouth

they pluck speech then reason   from me the maw-ma

because *quenched is the speaking water also*

after a long & intense conditioning   of me alone

vestal drones fasting   to practice pity or pith

sisters *know thyself*

others can you maybe   operate my tassel   rub up on the fodder

for I may be   dilly-dallying in the antechamber

shoving plants   up my shelf   beforehand

The Virus About Us

Many believe this spell   accentuates the end

of felting   on earth

where woeful band of scraggly whatnots

cling to life on sets   A plane of implications

      erupts in a species   evidenced by decreasing codices

Riddles I spew   loop in honor   of our most moat—

while the whimpering   king   spoons   a necrotic past.

Tripod Lockdown

Celibacy is my zone guys
fasting alone
via literate hoodlums

supported by loam sisterhood
scholars will wander
at the elevated vulva.

Bow to appalling instrument
or a plectrum
that makes speech

& applaud earth with gawkers
so I may be upright
on the hyped-up tripod

that emanates herb fumes
the pneuma tithing either
as gas or water.

Plutarch thought
emissions
weaken wordplay
but I am dancer sweet
& my sweat stature
blazes the turntable.

Watch my lips hit the pipe—
whoa it razzles my crotch
wherein cradled in the mtnscape
thesauri dot
future stairways.

Antediluvian Floozy

Man has it been
a long *long* time
since we pinched
out the bar Atlantis
into a serious party region
of wicked street buskers
where amused fans first rose
from the barbershop state
dove into cheesy regencies
& took a ton of lawn chairs
until our nipple civilization
became a course of ages
overflowing shores
thus at the dart board
a true answer died
leaving in the world
a mess of gardens
now aligning us
my precious cornichons.

The Pythia Proudly Has ADHD

The world   Offed its spring
Offspring   Offered
Spring   Of spring
& all   & all
& all   I said was

When the General Arrives w/His Ask

Whoa I shove a well
into yr nostrils
while you mine
mine & swipe right.

Let's second that dial-a-story
where I am the teller
& every glint is so ridic

it grinds solar eclipses
into concentric bands.
I caucus for toy scapes.

Then rake you a zodiac
replete w/cosmic blowouts.
For I certainly do not hoard

any phrase that exposes yr
divestment from
an awaiting universe.

Make Love Not Wall

Dude   deep in yr
frontal lobe

a brawny   torch
reboots trampolines.

Having now applied
the illusion theory

we have stopped
carving disputes

so that healing begins.
Sophisticated friend images

visit, sends the writer bums in,
having burned today's stargate.

As the dead figure docks
rebellious types w/

neoprene headdresses
shucked from the great flood

rise rise rise
in the king's chamber.

Made of royal cubits
I assess the structure

of seven bloodstained suns
& gypsum fun.

The gods always face
as if they're looking out

—therefore set
additional seal stones

which leads us hotties
to remembering

a natural rock-
hard ontology.

Wait   let's not
lose the target

& apply this
to the other,

the wetter side
of the palace.

Shhh @the Temple of Inscriptions

Dear   stellar dentata   take position

    as verses drive   the vehicle

Vaporize the evidence   set gold teeth   .

    against a poison of origins

Remove yr grill   from my mug

    nosing around   my other clavicle

So glissando   until nothing   controls the levers

    beside us   several nozzles glaze on

I can't see it mang   the kinghead cries

    inside an unidentifiable object

Major drat   I mean   are you down or not

w/my hunkering jowls   of serpent

The Age of Nefarious

Well, we'll thank you

whence delivering
an understanding
via tribal octaves

tell us what's inside
that secreting
diamond

or risk groaning
in the garden.

Do us a favor
as we fiddle w/unfriending
any venom-laced investment.

Like pros
we choke out
the auras haunting
the planetary chariot.

If you moon us
w/yr stupidity
an unknown
gold will take you—

Hurry up vax up
so that for realz

we can go clubbing
& keep hustling Aquarians
to light the fires.

Queen of the Night

I have captured the scattered animals,
bent innumerable heads a bit
& tilted their precious arms.

To some I gave a rhombus, an ode,
to others dejection, a human shape.

The coliseum dominates the state—
panels stymied by stars,

ribbed w/lodestone. Macromind
a constant in constellations.

Comets of comments
tally the galaxy.

Tales interstice the colony. Language
differentials & a celestial identity

descend down human tunnels,
the shaft a specialty. The shaft

an able body, an emptying vessel
making an attempt at understanding.

But a nocturnal continuum
insists we are dreamers.

The moon is known as a hardening effect by the children of fire.
The aria leads the lovers astray, tripping w/desire.

Mycenae, Founded by Fungi

My throat sends an alert.
The mushroom-picker has come.

Thirsty, he will make his pruning hook a divining rod
shaking it all the way to the citadel.

The site a sight.
A citation of the city's ages & usages.

Beneath that, my subterranean spring adores a discovery
for it to flush & flow once more.

When Perseus confronts the mooing sisterhood, we hiss & moo.
A pentatonic scale, the lowing of the cattle our sound.

We call the moon down, relatedly Io.
This type of plucking will be conducive to his purse.

Depending on the substrate, the matter & habit
determine how much bloodletting will ensue.

The lions indicate a femaleness.
A foreign name refounds the town:

Mystae, even. *Mykes* in Greek.
Mukānai, Mykenes, My keys.

Willingly I let go of my head.
I may never forgive the man

who faltered & fulfilled his oracle,
he who let the cap fall off his own head.

Visions of the city all around him.
His thirst a replacement for wonder.

Poly Colony

Long after the volcano,
programmed violence remains.

But what has happened to our new
friend, collecting saffron?

Assembled from the shattered
painting, she is dateable

shards latent from the disaster, complete
with stamens in the hands of the younger.

What was was swept away from the ash—
the soot a suite for a contemporary decade.

She knows the secret of the crocus &
its menstrual code. Her pain a satellite.

The ancient paint an ochre, a coveted pace.
That lacks an insistence of content.

Still I labor
over these fragments. They portray

an idea of gathering. Of corpus
doused w/togetherness.

For the island was once a clod
of dirt carried at the core of the lovers for days.

Every layer of the ejecta dismantling time,
every emittance a proposal.

Pleasure Centaur

Let pressure release
the unnamable ones

wobbling the tales
I tally   as senses deviate

Saturn loses
its rondeau wardrobe.

We begin to see
the crying ever over

snow-tired trilobites
fossil-mounting pinecones

or nautilus shell.
If naught for them

I spool fools
of the globe   we

glob around   I spit
out geometric codes

& say   fondle me by
contemplating roads

essential to the education
of active underwear.

Vestals Hack the Passcode

Bathed in the soft light
the snake tech

teaches us the wayward
winepress where

sots holla to strap up
our hot stuff boots

while we fluff wisemen
into a fiery powder.

For we the felines adorn
a dedicated entry

& guarantee the seekers
the right to invisible helpers.

Totes everything is a matter
of capitulation or copulation

but don't bereave
don't leave—
let's link tits

to resist
this atrocious composition.

The Feisty Disc Discovery

Find mine   I beg you

surrounded in lost smoke
while I hound rare peridot

& mount the unknown:

a language
open now for hot
deciphers until

ancient puncture
—remember it

consists of a sap quality
akin a jade chamber

so just tap yr fingers
to stoke a honey plot

plugging one end
the other in production

of bracketed glyphs
still lips   loop a sinker

deafening outside
my unburied orgasm.

New Dating Technique

—As I have answered so many times—
whenever I start the talk—sacred records rock out
remembering raw ziggurats—correlating
a delay of weather w/lunar groupings—

Don't admonish this response
—I mean it's heavy but ancient
timekeepers guarded stone observatories
& calculated periods

—Bloody as hell—the word meaning
blessings—but whether such shrine is ready
whether we shot up pure meds or not—we need
a new dating technique—

A reckoning of phrases
over loud displays of cock probs—
—remain to be calculated—

We revolve around
the calendar baton—fibula-like &
quartz-tipped—accompanied by grooves
it dates back to the Schwag Dynasty—

Take this stick—do yourself a favor
suck on it—we—are out of dictated
time—Let me tell you
the notches are my moon nominations—

score if you can—take them out for debate
—panting they are ready
for centuries—to incite

our united erection of rhyme.

Mistress of Honey

I do I do

live in
dream time

thoughts consumed
by the mystery

wherein the mute
can hear both
a distant noise

& a subsuming
declaration

or any emerging
note

an antibacterial
skin seal
from the mom canal

Did the pastors know
if they spent

any significant
mind sleeping

that the living
would convert

& don shirts
of a pleated & mtn'd
cognition

a habit as incongruous
as the pineal expulsion
when dreaming

a model
of the groin
in the dose

Did they plan
for the symbol

avatars to
discover
the keyhole
& stick fingers
in it

flicking
a switch
as we subsist
w/in the mini veils

We smushed
up on the access
holographic
of the idea itself

the battery in hand
gelid at first—

then a bee
shaking its pollen
leg pouch

after it
entered the center

gently inserting
nectar into
an office

like a word
makes mud

mutable
for the nest
by vibrating

How a Bill Originates in Vulvic Space

Whaddya know according to the peeps
the world began w/a question—
which is helpful since we all lost track
of the task of wonder.

In dictating doozies of the polity
include the dates of awkward shipments
include the ovary foil that lines pyramids
made libel by the security company.

For the oldest zodiac parts the boundary
so oily it turns into a sea of cataracts
labeled in ivory jars stored for initiates.

Upon viewing the bribes
of so-&-so let the record show
legends & breastplates stuttering in puddles.

The king is collecting enemies of the
upper & lower sunsets
collapsing his raspy tongue.

Answers conspire around
my velvet anvil & stars tink
to shake a solar boat
into denoting hope.

Therefore   once more
I totally touch myself
to make the blank & blank appear.

Animous   Uni State
erased from the Declaration of Independence

When   the   human   becomes   one
                                        bands connect   them
the powers of the earth   equal station to   laws of nature
nature's God   entitle them
respect   kind
they impel   truths to be   self   created   endowed   Creator
with certain   alien   life   happiness.

Deriving their just powers from ends   is the right   institute
new foundation   to effect   safety
indeed   changed experience   disposed to right   selves
by abolishing forms
A long train   pursuing invariably   the same   design
Absolute.

It is their right, it is their duty, to guard their future patient   colonies;
and such is now   the necessity
to alter form system
The history   present   is a history of   direct   states.
To prove this   candid   assent to   wholesome   good.

Forbidden   operation   assent   obtained;   and
    so utterly   attend
accommodation   districts   relinquish representation
formidable   called together   bodies   places unusual   distant
depository of   records   measure   dissolved   houses
    opposing   firmness.

Exercise   time exposed   to invasion from without
convulsions within   endeavored   population;
migration hither   raising the conditions
Will alone   erected a multitude of new   swarms
their substance   peace — independent   power
combined with   others   large bodies of   us:

protecting   inhabitants of these states: all parts of the world:
imposing   us   consent: cases of benefits   transporting us
    beyond seas to:
free   province   establishing   therein — enlarging its boundaries

so as to render   fit instrument   absolute   colonies:
altering fundamentally the forms   declaring   selves
power to legislate protection — our seas   our coasts   towns and
    lives.

Time   transporting large   complete works   parallel   ages
    total   head

Fellow citizens take   captive the high!   Country   become
    friends and brethren
hands   endeavored to bring on the inhabitants of our frontiers
                of all ages   sex   conditions
Every stage   humble   petitions
    answered only by
prince character   marked   act   of a free   people.

We have been wanting   time to extend   over us.

We have reminded them of the circumstances of our settlement here.
We have appealed to native   we have conjured   hem ties of our
    kindred vow
inevitably our connections   correspond   to the voice of
    justice and o
We must   hold them   as we hold   kind   peace friends.

We   representatives of the assembled Supreme   world   Name
united colonies   right ought   free   absolved from all
Crown   all   connection between them   and
Great   Divine Providence
we mutually pledge   Light

Lady with a Lamp

Florence Nightingale, Crimea, 1854

Fire, somehow, lodged in shadows. Fire on thy father's thighs that
    prompted a birth.
Fire in labor's sweat, sweet in labor. Fire in my hair,
    just as the reports report.

Fire from Prometheus, transported narthex, fire in the *thyrus* firing.
    Fire when I greet you. Firelight the time you called—notes I
scrawled, made by you.

Beloved, fire in the gift at age twelve. Fire in the eternity-like eight
    you behold.
Fire alerting swabs I arrange. In the kitchen, the nursing preparations.

Fire   heat   finer   scour   fire ours   to repeat.

I visit the sick as instructed, lantern in my hands, firing lamplight to
    illuminate the rooms—
stereoscopic ceiling, a ship flaring *Exit* if they exhume. Fire a virus
    I can burn through.

Hemoglobin a nest of balloons, honeycomb of embers. Fire in
    the truth I wander after.
Fire searing when I touch the wounds, each a matrix
    aflame. They won't wane.

Fire of the destroyer, welding this war. Fire on my tongue, the
    weary soldier's scorch.
When I touch the men, they mistake me for a floating angel:

One writes letters about kissing my shadow, seen stretching over
    pillows. Waiting behind his
horror, behind my body, the Source. *Good Lord*, allow me an

adjustment of the canopy

in my hands. Find my smock. Reach in for the cloth. Each soak a god
    in motion & here is a
gesture, an unforgotten salve. My master, unscathe us. Apply to me
    a resonant bandage.

Make me the school I will name after St. Thomas. I'll administer
    as I did on Nysa, old
island where we nippled thousands. Give to me volumes
    on philosophy & religion.

Fire in my sight even as I lose it. Fire in our recognition,
    the recognition, our medicine.

We All Need a Death Doula

The dead woman has come down from
the ozone hills. Her child is walking with her.
It is the child killed by pandemic, before
the war, before the want.

A copper tone anoints. They are both candles
having allowed the human life to be harsh.
Grape touched, her leopard camisole cannot come off.
Her reed basket made of fronds, not food.

When the rain comes, it will come as insulation.
A dog day, a mage, a derision
of cicada song. Long disintegrated from the shadow,
the original pilots have no say, no existence here.

A spirit that is left skates around them
& instructs on toward the marsh: the plants
indicate first a paper future, then absorption of outlaws.

Out of a freezer, DNA is removed
to continue. Robes are there, domineering
in show. Proliferation is a meadow
found when a contagion last dangled in the well.

I am staggering under the hive, donning a green
headband & leather claws. Yet there is another body—
the half-buried jug of wine, waiting
to open. I touch the mother, we hand over
the reports; prepare the swing to put the child in.

Over the open pit, censors adjust an smoke element.
A haunting may end in the upper world.

Elegy for a Satyr

under searchlights   skulking beneath

beams   we drowned   in music

grasping onto   the stacks

slapping shapes   past us   brewing storms   bidding

covered bridges   their best—   hooking you yr rest

lanterns   beers   buoy   goatboy correspondence

amidst designs   releasing traffic lights

from the dancing ground

yr hug humpy   pranic breath   in ear

our embouchure muscular   body prison of the heart

onto us   an architecture you drew

speaker wind-absolved   pillars   shaped labrys

quickly fashion a ship did we   a heavy sealant reveals a new

mystery—my misery   accessing the median

then let depression take over   earth opens   one slit in skin

Saint Pain bring to us   an offering at intermission

so we will relinquish   a sturdy tether

unbidden hilarity   fuck this   feeble disease

free the boat from its rope   warping   wounds

dangling string from wonder   do you stumble starman

dammit why didn't you tell us   wolfbrother

yr dogs also in the inflatable   tube not far behind   us   now

a log hewn for the ride   down   the river

let's call it   a labor day   caulking   unclenched

released from yr overalls   from yr t-shirt of a tree

now then   we'll come to yr extraction

a skipper's sudden   entrance & exit

Fancy Necromancy

Let's apprehend the illicit   initiate who
slobbers on the sacred pimp cup, dishonoring   a generative drink.

Faux lord, stop snoring   in the courts   of the impulse kingdom.
Don a sovereign shroud   or die in this campaign   of laden thunder.

Solemn avatars,   let's triple the sounds   & hire lotuses
to stoke the meter   after we rid the grid   of old agony

Give head   way to the dancers   on the confirmation floor,
while friends fingerblast   farms into radiance.

For if you accost us again, we will be rearing our dead
& raising them onward.

Dollar Goddess

One question still unresolved is:
Who is the money dead person

depicted being kind on that
famed sarcophagus? Well it

is for sure universally identified
as the spirit of a dead stewardess.

Let's open that credenza

& coincidentally re-cunt
that man-hero standing

in the way of our tomb
understanding.

Helmet Dressing Room

once the objects said
vote for the proper codes

my outer triangle
insisted on
advancing a shell

so yo
spiral yr own

axis from plane
to pupil

may-eye
follow you back

ditching crowns
but what about
yr pinecone

noose of
ripped diamonds

crip up dimension
to let it shine

let it shrine
this little tetrahedron

of mine

How to Haul a Parasol

For rapt observatory
of turnt up crown

rupture open
a receptor

while I don
waterfall serifs

Maybe ask
you out

over a lid of
half waves

then get lit
milking hairbrushes

feel up a mushroom
'til it obeys abodes

unknot a clod
clad in ditches

Come come home
while cornea dons

a whipped chariot
or is it albedo

I guess when
yr hooded robe

yanks I shuck it
& we hit up a

void stadium
so lampshades rib out

to paste batter
against crappy basins

& I parachute
onto yr tripod

where achy
mtn basket

overturns dials
into towering harmonies

then socket a
look-out

For fucksake
find a natal chart

. drenched in
scalloped lenses

of marbleized cones
so ponds

touch & attempt
to settle a hypostyle

Hells ya thank
the first element

a parabolic cloud
that battens down

all obelisks
Oh! there goes

the door-knocking
porter who lodges

megaphones to hug
our wakened face

Whistle Blow Her

Say we have come
here on a dream
threatening to bust out
our brooms & dress-up
in rotating crops.

Or insist we shake
en route to night
while flesh brews
in the mystery ballots.

Or suggest a pinner
of the latest aphrodisiac
to discover any awestruck
nose as booster seat
for sex medication.

See that they saw a log
promoting stewardship.
Then bangarang! We
are killin' it w/the quest.

Such that the rotting relatives
can no longer ignore
songs cresting
in our throats.

Joan d'Arc

Once, a prediction of fire.
Before that, the undying presence of names.
Keepers, flare.
Look footward, there
the depth a death
the unseen thatching itself.
Will will open open up—
self-direct one way
seal over knit gather repair
pearl in the phosphorus.
Made to turn into the other,
wrangle in the slashed reeds.
What a heart we have here:

Soggy Augury

Despite these tweaks of the machine the breeze is message-less.

I throw sleepless tokens & pulp armpit energy

to instruct num-nums toward banned ruins.

But uttering into dens I befriend any trending echo

& throw ashes onto its soundboard to bear a giant luck.

When the coven needs a new oven, I craft an emoji

w/spigots of chronic froth. I hit the matrix for protection,

make a junket from suburbs soaked in color. Blackouts beware.

I saturate reading to bring stakeholders to their knees.

For our hunky-dory skeletons skirmish for one

epic hard-on—so the really regal spirits

will finally articulate our blockhead heart.

Labyrinth in Sync

Lyre maiden   weirdo dancer
I address my creature stature   I accept myself

warped as I am   grabbing a hashtag outta   group grope.
In it   the lost formula   of a country   I repeatedly pet.

When the invaders come they won't
know I hit them w/a simulation system.

They won't fit   the frequencies   anymore.

Yet I tread the thread—heck I invented it
to lead us out of the cray. Along the way I slurp

up the preponderance of toxic bull & invoke
a hero   complete w/papyrus-charged gifts—

a weft oft ignored   by lame patriarchs
who cannot   get off   & instead go to war.

HMU@Emerald Tablets

In obedience w/the law
flower   ban any dweller

w/soft detachment
whose dowdy heart

needs to get stuffed.

Fiery I often respond
while the world blobs

of disordered waters
& streams cast live

from the temples,
(are you watching yet?)

of which so few are left—
that we attempt

to chunk out info
against total horror.

So YOLO   we rose
in the ship of the matter.

Altered the intel
each host a cast spell.

Gathered I my people
ye gatherers   totally

gather ye   together.

For the sons   must change
direction of the great flame

but no worries—
raging   crones arrive

& take a knuckle of earth
w/cudgels & consume it.

Yes, you should cower
by my display of magi-science.

For emissary of earth am I
I swelter again & again

then blast us a path to
reset Truth

into the records.

WTF @the Library of Alexandria

Handiwipes
by my side

I'm the lead librarian
on this clean-up job

so: smear my breath
open up the bellows

cool down
the new glands
key the beast
or marine drama

but study the empire
while I sweep up this heap.

In stride w/the bunker of the sun
I arrange the columns
& eat any leftover stash

while latent watchers
detect a satellite
powered by charred
endocrine.

You seethe—
every shaft is talking to us

echolocation of ruins
modify my mop & syllabus.

Comrade, salve all over
the theater of anatomy

bronze a healing center
dangle in the bathysphere

go bonkers at the gym
be staid at the stadium

not to mention elevate
an illogical
botanical garden

wherein we achieve
human completion.

When I arrive in hazmat
yr shelves   have dreamt

of me & so we beg
any remnant scrolls
to bleed   exquisitely.

Duende Friending

She will split if you wait
no face but the gaze finale
her address   chaparral
near Plato's pad   near
urine & lilies
coal bin body
her clothes barrels   doulas
wrinkles   vigil-stained   dreams
learn to ride   a sign says
I'm a driving child
foreplay in the vile
She animal me animal
the nurse at work mashing molecules
not to maim mother   blemish ish
damaged bed of leaves
other places   doubt palaces
but donning bull hide
then   she   pigeon claw
She   friend to wind
kernels of   the tactile
whose screen are we
still we stare 'til engines start
fey light & digits
marrow roused
look of blood   under her
She'll spit if you wait
see chains   hear strings
syncing   I'm a pump
of impurities quake ready
are those buds or nipples
pushing up pastures
offer of vandalized eyes
if you won't dance w/me
why are you here

Pythia LOL

OMG—I know those words spit out at you
    May confuse a tune but
    C'mon, I never hoard them;
      My boo, praise generous fumes
      Seducing me *hahaha* to
    Fork over those few—

W*i*T*C*h Please

Come back, we need you.
Remember in Lemuria
we were living memory

we kept posterity active
in the reflective ether

having scraped resin
we mated to
see the epics volt the synaptic mess.

Ommmming out many tokes
to take us into shape.

Lucky us, later the labyrinth
became a club complete w/
a renovated dancing ground.

We found therein
all the tincture
& a glyph-deciphering kit.

We dusted
for fingerprints.
For whorl recognition.

We sold off statues
to speak to each other
w/out speaking.

So could you be so kind
as to visit this site
hold hands & download this link—
looping our mother back to us.

Pentheus the Unelected

You're fired, say I, your mother-maenad, Agave.
For the *thiasos* is a band *and* a dance—
We let it all hang out, circle round,
Worship a could-be bone relic
The size of a pea
A pinecone centers in a tiny cave,
Lodged above the hormone pit stop,
Which retires behind the nose's root.
It wires color eye after eye,
Attached to a third rail, w/vents at least
To the oppressed mind.
Are you afraid yet? Yr clan banned
The function of this masked gland,
Long told to be our connection to the Realms of Thought—
But more active at night, so what? Call us swingers, huh,
But just for the doubling light.
We circle round, hexing scoundrels who mangle the seat.
Thrum a pulse at the base of the brain, prodded by our troupe,
Not by toupee. Touché. This gland is so rad.
An organ of talents. An adulterer of states.
They will say I wasn't awake, exactly,
When you were caught spying on us, a woody throng.
But no worries. I'll activate the area anyway,
Circle round with sisters,
Then I slay yr neck & paw on,
lobbing yr head off, aloft beyond my crime.

Aliens, Do Arrive Pronto

Apologies for that old pole shift.
But Avebury, you here? Egypt?
Reps from Bimini Road, are you here?
Azores, yo. Moundbuilders, we missed you.
Sumerians, 'sup? Nvm the Mayans erupted
& the Anasazi disappeared—
you "people" present? We never collected
yr minutes, Pleiadians, but welcome.
Remote Minoans, hello.
Will brother Orpheus-the-charmer show up?
First order, take this *kykeon* bowl, this wide spaceship
to drink from, hold the bull horns
& guzzle against the pain; thwart the
architects inhaling a chemical muse.
Swill on. Then take out the ambassador trash.
Saint Civ, let's commence.

Rock on Parnassos

They came down
from higher ground

foraged minerals
& misled the

menace insisting
on answers

trying to fire
the questions

but boulders rolled
peak to belly

the plateau nestled
talking crags

as far-flung bands
of stars had fallen

tidbits stressed
pillared ruins

tripod pieces
spurned the chasm

where the steam
is plasma music

& underground
steam or notes

now go stoking
the holy bodies.

The Pythia's Final Prophecy

I shed my cave when we buried the banned kings and soddened their derelict futures. We started as archetypes and had fun with readings. Then the new cult co-opted our *apophenia*, making connections that aren't there. The poets will be so pissed. Here at the oracle, we bulk up on shots, suggesting a twist in plot. Those crowding the dancing grounds are wasted symbols. Bodies gone. I inscribe oak leaves for correct action, but they are trash. The bills shall be sacrificed. But be careful about the intoxication. There's the earth type, magic plant, or fumes kind, then there's another drunkenness—that of the market. Apollo is a fossil fuel. Its sun shunts the serpent. Under python, the major navel, holy *omphalos*. This type of center means it deliberates, isn't digital. It morphs on and on. So, sparks, ping me then paste a clit icon to your endless calendar.

Self-Love

I said to the healer
I am lustful for dear country
—or is it a *company*—
to acquire a medicine bag.

I said to the hookup,
let's invent the bullroarer
and decolonize percussion.
For up until the inquisition
we ate out prime molecules
at every sundry palace.

So then I said to the headmaster
the greater the pain
the better the sweep
of stakeholders' remains.

I said to my lung, hang on—
all you have to do is
flub the flower in me
& send signals
to the shoulder corridors.

My head said to me:
If every click is a foreplay
just heart it & then crash
the shopping carts
to agitate & emit
an antiseptic defense

such as thumbing iambs
into a crafty honing device
that replaces the horrible suffering.

Acknowledgments

I AM SO GRATEFUL for the music, syllabic tool and source of the non-sense. And to my family, who believe my work deserves discovery. Without you, there would be no words.

This book is indebted to the art of Hilda Doolittle, Diane DiPrima, Isadora Duncan, Eva Palmer Sikelineos, and the work of Jane Ellen Harrison, Marija Gimbutas, and Maria Reiche. Through myth and ritual, these women re-membered matriarchy and thus our ability to exit patriarchy.

There is no accurate acknowledgment for what is owed to the places roped off for me to dig: Abenaki land and the Vermont Studio Center, Meskwaki and Sauk and Iowa lands, Northern Michigan land of the Anishinaabek, The Community of Writers, Cahuilla territory, and indigenous Oregon. And deep gratitude to Portland respites that encouraged this work: Elise Schumock and her Rose City Book Pub, and Ally Harris and the Submission Reading Series. And to poet Rachel Abramowitz, thank you for encouraging me to ruin around in Greece (even after our trip).

Cleveland State University Press, PANK, and Fonograf Editions also heartened these poems via their book contests. Candace Williams, Julie Scelfo, and Dr. Richard Norris all helped with submission fees—those small gestures mean everything.

I also owe a great deal to my early poetry mentors: JoAnn O'Hern, Nick Bozanic, Edward Hirsch, and LeAnne Howe. And for Brenda Hillman and Robert Hass, thank you for your activism and animism. Poems can rise at the Nevada Test Site, (while the Shoshone, the Temple of Sekhmet, and the Nevada Desert Experience rematriate the land). Poetry *is* a relic.

A sequined gratitude to the excavators of my poetry life: Claudia Keelan, Donald Revell, the University of Nevada Press, *Interim Poetics* staff, and its editorial board: Ronaldo Wilson, Sasha Steensen, and Sherwin Bitsui, thank you!

What a wonderful boon I received from the publications where these poems first appeared: "Aurora" appeared in *Tight* (2008); "The Last Venue" originally published as "Hammer", *interrupture*, a journal of poetry and art (Winter, 2010);

"How a Bill Originates in Vulvic Space" appeared in *TYPO* (Issue 27, 2017); "Tripod Lockdown" originally published as "Adyton," *Wave Composition* (Issue 10, September 2015); "Helmet Dressing Room" appeared in *Wave Composition* (Issue 10, September 2015); "Duende Friending," originally published as "You Who Zula," *Coldfront Magazine* (January 2014); "Lady with a Lamp" appeared in *Interim Poetics* (Spring 2014); "We All Need a Death Doula" originally published as "Erigone," *Interim Poetics,* (Spring 2014); "Mistress of Honey" originally published as "Diophilia," *H_ngm_n* (Spring 2012); "Mycenae, Founded by Fungi" originally published as "Mycenae," *H_ngm_n,* (Spring 2012); "Animous Uni State" appeared in *Occupy Poetry* (January 2012); "Queen of the Night" appeared in *Colorado Review,* (vol. 38.1, Spring 2011); "Joan d'Arc" appeared in *Badlands* (vol. 1.1, Summer 2010); "Poly Colony originally published as "Thera," *The Equalizer* (vol. 1.1, January 2009); "Rock on Parnassos" originally published as "Parnassus," *venusrisingmagazine.com* (vol. 32, no. 4, 2009). And thanks to WFMU's Frow Show for casting some into audio collage.

About the Author

KATHERINE FACTOR is an editor, book coach, and educator. She was the writer-in-residence at Idyllwild Arts and Interlochen Arts academies, and has an MFA in poetry from the University of Iowa Writers' Workshop. Factor is a recipient of grants from the Iowa Arts Council and the Arts Enterprise Laboratory for publishing young writers. She is the author of three Choose Your Own Adventure books—*Spies: Mata Hari; Spies: Harry Houdini;* and *Spies: Spy for Cleopatra.*